YOU
GET ME

GARY CHAPMAN & JEN MICKELBOROUGH

YOU GET ME

SIMPLE, ROMANTIC WAYS
TO SPEAK THE 5 LOVE LANGUAGES®

NORTHFIELD PUBLISHING
CHICAGO

Artwork by Jen Mickelborough
Edited by Elizabeth Cody Newenhuyse
Interior and cover design: Erik M. Peterson
Cover and interior illustrations by Jen Mickelborough

Library of Congress Cataloging-in-Publication Data
Names: Chapman, Gary, author. | Mickelborough, Jen, author.
Title: You get me : simple, romantic ways to speak the 5 love languages /
   Gary Chapman and Jen Mickelborough.
Description: Chicago : Northfield Publishing, 2021. | Includes
   bibliographical references. | Summary: "In You Get Me, find simple,
   practical ideas for how to infuse your relationship with excitement,
   joy, and intimacy as you love your beloved in the ways that mean the
   most to him or her. From planning spontaneous dinners to warm embraces,
   learn ways to communicate your love in every love language"-- Provided
   by publisher.
Identifiers: LCCN 2020039926 (print) | LCCN 2020039927 (ebook) | ISBN
   9780802422682 (paperback) | ISBN 9780802499424 (ebook)
Subjects: LCSH: Interpersonal relations. | Marriage. | Love.
Classification: LCC HM1106 .C4843 2021 (print) | LCC HM1106 (ebook) | DDC
   302--dc23
LC record available at https://lccn.loc.gov/2020039926
LC ebook record available at https://lccn.loc.gov/2020039927

We hope you enjoy this book from Northfield Publishing. Our goal is to provide high-quality, thought-provoking books and products that connect truth to your real needs and challenges. For more information on other books and products that will help you with all your important relationships, go to northfieldpublishing.com or write to:

Northfield Publishing
820 N. LaSalle Boulevard
Chicago, IL 60610

1 3 5 7 9 10 8 6 4 2

Printed in the United States of America

In loving memory of David Andrew
1975–2019
Big brother, listener, encourager.
First of our generation, he will always be missed.

INTRODUCTION

JEN

I wrote the first version of this book in a little spiral-bound notepad sixteen years ago, in the first year of our marriage. My husband's (Fran's) great act of love to me was renovating our house from top to bottom, but actually what I wanted was to take a walk together, to go for a coffee, or sit and snuggle while we watched TV—simple, everyday ways to connect and feel loved.

When we made our vows, we were happy and earnest but had no idea of the work, commitment, and service that would be involved. But we learned, and are still learning. For us, these simple gestures have either been the icing on the cake in good times, or created a climate of love and tenderness in the tough times. When they've been neglected, our connection has suffered. When they've been invested in, our connection has flourished—they've helped unite us. The little things can make a big difference, and I encourage you to try it too. If your relationship is thriving, try it and see the joy multiply. If your relationship is struggling, try it and see connection and tenderness grow as you invest in meeting your partner's love needs.

GARY

Perhaps you have read the original book, *The 5 Love Languages®: The Secret to Love That Lasts,* and are familiar with the five love languages. If not, here is the basic concept and a brief description of the love languages. Most of us assume that what makes us feel loved will also communicate love to someone else. That is a false assumption. What I (Gary) discovered in counseling couples is that each of us has a primary love language, and if we don't receive love in that language, we will not feel loved. So, the wife says, "I feel like you don't love me." The husband responds, "How could you say that? I wash your car every Saturday, I vacuum on Thursday nights, and help you with the laundry. Why would you not feel loved?" The answer is simple. While she appreciates those acts of service, that is not her primary love language. She feels loved when you take walks with her or have an extended conversation with her. The husband is sincere, but he is missing her emotionally. So here is a brief description of the five love languages.

WORDS OF AFFIRMATION—using words to express appreciation and gratitude. "You look nice in that outfit." "One of the things I appreciate about you is . . ." The words may focus on the way the person looks, a personality trait, something they have done for you, or their positive attitude.

QUALITY TIME—giving the person your undivided attention. This can be done over a meal or simply sitting on the couch for an extended conversation. It may be doing a project together, such as planting a flower garden. The important thing is not what you are doing but that you are doing it together. This was the primary love language of the lady noted above who wanted to take walks with her husband.

GIFTS—giving gifts is a universal expression of love. The gift says, "They were thinking about me. Look what they got for me." The gift need not be expensive. Haven't we always said, "It's the thought that counts"? If this is the other person's primary love language, then gifts will speak deeply of your love.

ACTS OF SERVICE—doing something for the other person that you know they would like for you to do. This is spoken in such things as cooking meals, washing dishes, walking the dog, etc. This is the language the husband noted above was speaking in washing her car, vacuuming, and helping with the laundry. The old saying "Actions speak louder than words" is true if Acts of Service is their love language.

PHYSICAL TOUCH—affirming touches that say, "I love you." Parents speak this language when they hold and cuddle their baby.

In marriage, this includes such things as holding hands, kissing, hugging, or sitting close to each other as you watch a movie.

Out of these five, each of us has a primary love language. One speaks more deeply to us emotionally than the other four. If we don't speak the other person's primary love language, they will not feel loved, even though we are speaking some of the other languages. This explains why we can be sincere but still miss each other emotionally.

Don't hear me saying that we should speak *only* their primary love language. We give heavy doses of the primary and then sprinkle in the other four for "extra credit." The other languages are more meaningful if we are consistently receiving love in our primary language. The purpose of this book is to give you illustrated ideas on how to speak each of the five love languages.

HOW TO USE THIS BOOK

It's simple—just start trying out the different ideas! You might find it helpful to set a regular reminder on your phone to try one. Some may take a little more planning, like booking a restaurant or finding an attraction to visit, but many can be acted on or put into action without any additional work. If you're not sure what your partner's primary love language is, don't worry—there's a simple way to find out. One of the best ways to find your love language and your partner's is for the two of you take the free 5 Love Languages profile assessment at 5lovelanguages.com. Or you may also decide to just try the ideas presented in this book and note your partner's response—was it positive, neutral, or negative? Don't forget that all five love languages can be meaningful to them and that the way they receive love may change depending on the circumstances of their life at any given time.

At the back of the book, you'll find some pages where you can note:

- when you try an idea
- how it goes
- any variation you might try
- an asterisk column for your partner to mark ideas that would mean a lot to them

There are also some blank pages where your partner can add any ideas that would be particularly meaningful to them. We've included variations on ideas so you can choose what feels most natural to you or where budget or time availability may affect what you're able to do.

Our hope is that you will find these suggestions simple to put into action and that you will reap great rewards in the benefits to your relationship. May your love grow, deepen, and flourish as you find simple and meaningful ways to express your love to your partner.

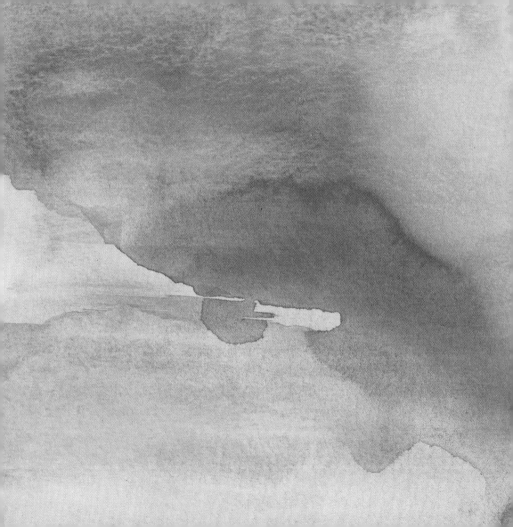

WORDS OF AFFIRMATION

1. POETRY OF LOVE

Write them a poem. Find a poem that
expresses your love or makes you
think of them. Buy a poetry book that
reminds you of them.

2. SURPRISE NOTE

Hide a note thanking them for how
they help you and love you under their pillow,
slipped into their bag, or in their drawer to be found
later.

3. JUST BECAUSE

Call or text them, just because you're thinking of them.

4. HANDMADE

Make a card for them. Anything from stick men or simple lettering to a more elaborate creation can convey a heartfelt message. Or help the kids make a card.

5. BODY BEAUTIFUL

Tell them what you love about their body.

6. PUBLIC PRAISE

Praise them in a public or social situation.

7. FRAME A LOVE MESSAGE

Give them a visual reminder of how you feel. Use an expression, quote, or a line from a poem if you need help with words.

8. COMPLIMENT THEIR APPEARANCE

Be specific about what you love and why.

9. PARENTING PARTNERS

If you have children, compliment their parenting. Tell them what you appreciate and why.

10. DAILY AFFIRMATIONS

Give them a compliment every day for a month.

11. THANK THEM

Be intentional about thanking them for the jobs and chores they do.

12. I LOVE YOU

Tell them "I love you"—in person, as a note, as a text message—just declare those three special words!

13. ENCOURAGING WORDS

Send them a loving and supportive message when they're having a hard day.

14. INTERIOR DESIGN

Tell them something you love about their home décor choices.

15. EXTERIOR DECLARATION

Mow a love message into the lawn. Draw it in sidewalk chalk. Pressure-wash it into the patio. Hang a banner on their birthday. Leave a love message on their frosty car.

16. MR. POSTMAN

Send them a letter or postcard when you're away. Send one even if you're not.

17. THREE THINGS

Have their friends each write down three things they love about them, and present these encouragements as a gift.

18. BE THEIR CHEERLEADER

Send them a positive message when they have a big day at work or other challenge that day.

19. PASS IT ON!

Take note of the good things other people say about them and pass them on.

20. ENCOURAGE THEIR HOBBIES

Encourage them to invest in or take the next step with one of their interests.

21. MEANINGFUL WORDS

Write a sincere love message or buy a card expressing how you feel.

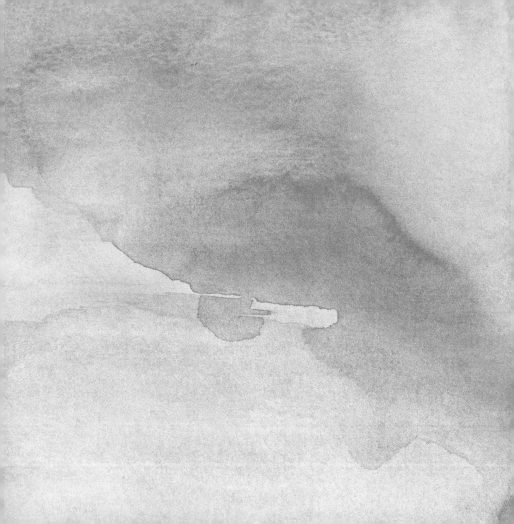

QUALITY TIME

1. PLAY A BOARD GAME TOGETHER

Have fun playing a game together. Borrow games from friends to try or visit a games café.

2. GET AWAY

Plan a weekend away for just the two of you. Take care of all the details (including childcare if needed). Plan a family outing or weekend trip if childcare is not available.

3. THE BIG QUESTIONS

Ask them about their life dreams.

4. COFFEE DATE

Take them out for coffee just to catch up on life or to make time for the big conversations that can be hard to fit in.

5. JOIN IN

Join one of their activities that you wouldn't normally do with them.

6. SWEET DREAMS!

Tuck them into bed at night.

7. DINING ALFRESCO

Take them on a picnic.
Pack sandwiches or visit
a deli and buy some treats.
Go at sunrise or sunset
with candles for a magical
touch.

8. GET ACTIVE

Try out a new sport together.

9. LISTEN TO THEIR WORRIES

Ask them how they're doing—take time to listen to how they're feeling (without trying to solve anything).

10. TAKE IN THE AIR

Sit in the yard or on the balcony on a nice evening. Take your meal outside and enjoy the space together.

11. LEARN TOGETHER

Take a class together.

12. UNPLUG

Turn off your phone and tablet for the evening, and give them your undivided attention.

13. NEW FLAVORS

Try a new restaurant or cuisine, or cook a new recipe together at home.

14. FIVE THINGS

Ask them for a list of five things they'd enjoy doing, then do one each month for the next five months.

15. EVENING TREAT

Take them to a dessert or cheese bar for an evening date, or just go out for an evening coffee.

16. **MOVIE NIGHT**

Find a movie you'd both love to watch together. Go out or snuggle up at home.

17. **EVENING STROLL**

Go for a relaxed evening walk together. Or take a bike ride!

18. **MYSTERY DATE**

Plan a secret date and surprise them with a night out. Arrange for a babysitter if needed.

19. TOURIST IN YOUR OWN TOWN

Visit a local garden, gallery, museum, or historic attraction together. Discover somewhere new, or share a place that's meaningful to one of you.

20. AS THE DAY ENDS

Make hot chocolate to share at the end of a long day, or spend time catching up over a special dessert just for the two of you.

21. IMPROMPTU DATE

If possible, invite them out for lunch spontaneously.

GIFTS

1. MISSING YOU

Bring back a gift from a business trip or after being away from home.

2. TWELVE DAYS OF GIFTS

Celebrate their birthday or your anniversary with twelve days of gifts.

3. WARM THEIR HEART

Buy them a snuggly scarf or gloves in cold weather.

4. THE GIFT THAT KEEPS GROWING

If you have a yard, plant their favorite tree, bush, or flowers. Or buy a small potted tree, and put it on your balcony.

5. THEIR OWN PERSONAL REGISTRY

Have them make an online gift list so you can buy them gifts spontaneously.

6. PHOTO MEMORIES

Print and frame a photo of the two of you together and present it to them.

7. SYMBOL OF LOVE

Hand-make a decorative heart for them. Try wood, collage, paints . . . Go to a craft store to get a base shape if needed.

8. TASTY TREATS

Buy one of their favorite treats when you shop for groceries. Bring home some baking, exotic fruit, or special chocolates for the weekend.

9. SHARED EXPERIENCE

Buy tickets to their favorite band/show/dance/comedian. Ask their friends or try something new if you have no idea.

10. FOUND TREASURES

Bring home wildflowers, beautiful leaves, pretty pebbles, or a striking feather from a walk for them.

11. YEAR AFTER YEAR

Decide together on a meaningful gift you both love for anniversaries to buy every year.

12. BORROWED EXPERTISE

Ask their friends for gift ideas. If you have kids, involve them in choosing a present.

13. LOVE IN BLOOM

Buy them flowers! Find out their favorite variety or colors. Buy a potted plant for long-lasting blooms.

14. THE GIFT THAT KEEPS ON GIVING

Buy them an online magazine or newspaper subscription or a membership to something they will enjoy.

15. YOUR SONG

Make a mix CD or playlist for them.

16. SURPRISE TREATS

Leave surprise treats somewhere they'll discover them.

17. THE ART OF LOVE

Buy a little artwork that reminds you of them or that you think they'll love.

18. INVEST IN THEIR INTERESTS

Buy them something that encourages their hobby.

19. GUILT-FREE INDULGENCE

Get them gift cards for something they wouldn't necessarily do for themselves—a spa treatment, sports event, their favorite small shop.

20. TAKE NOTE

Take note of something they like, and secretly buy it later as the perfect surprise gift.

21. THIRFTED TREASURES

Find a unique gift your partner would love—a specialist book, an interior decoration, or an accessory that matches their favorite outfit—all on a thrift store budget.

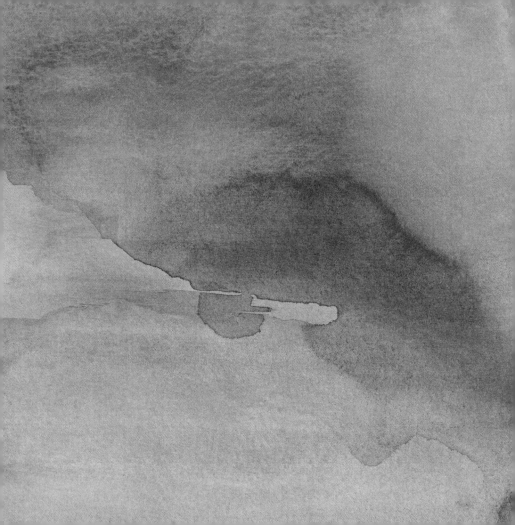

ACTS OF
SERVICE

1. CAR SERVICE

If you're handy, fix something in your partner's car. If you're not, take it to the car wash. Either way, they'll appreciate it!

2. LESSEN THE LOAD

Do one, some, or all of their chores for them. Or try sharing one of their chores—make it fun, put on some music, and have a laugh together.

3. TO THE RESCUE

Rescue them from some unpleasant task they've been putting off (cleaning a closet, taxes, weeding . . .). Do it yourself.

4. I.O.U.

Write a note pledging to do something for them today (and make sure you do it!).

5. READY FOR COMPANY!

Help tidy the house for visitors.

6. SNOW REMOVAL

Clear ice or snow off the path. Defrost or warm their car for them.

7. BREAKFAST IN BED

Make them tea or coffee in the morning. Bring them breakfast in bed on a special day.

8. SWEET RELIEF

Ease their aches and pains with a back, hand, or foot massage.

9. INVOLVED PARENT

If you have kids, be proactive about spending time with them. This could be anything from helping them with homework to shooting baskets in the driveway to taking them on a special outing.

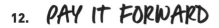

10. TECH SAVIOR

Fix their tech problems—or at the very least, call tech support so they don't have to.

11. DO THE DISHES

Clean up after dinner (if you're not the one this usually falls to).

12. PAY IT FORWARD

Do something that helps out someone they love.

13. BIRTHDAY BAKER

Make a cake for their birthday, or pick up one you know they would really like. Don't forget the ice cream!

14. NOURISH

Have dinner ready at the end of a long day. Make them sandwiches or a lunch bag for work.

15. TIME TO THEMSELVES

Encourage them to spend time doing something they love. Entertain the kids (or take them out) so they can take a nap.

16. FIRE OF LOVE

Light a fire for them. Leave their slippers out waiting for them on a cold day. Fill up their hot water bottle when they're cold.

17. RESTFUL ROOM

Make the bed, put your clothes away, clear up clutter. Make sure the bedroom is a peaceful space.

18. RUN INTERFERENCE

Make sure they can enjoy their favorite TV show in peace by taking care of interruptions for them.

19. PAPER PUSHER

Take care of the paperwork and/or bills.

20. HELP WITHOUT BEING ASKED

Don't wait until your partner makes a request. Surprise them and just do the chore.

21. RELIEF WORK

Find out which chore they most dislike and see how you can relieve them of that duty.

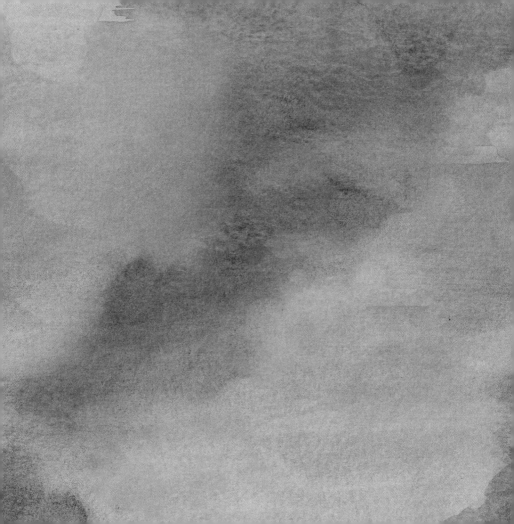

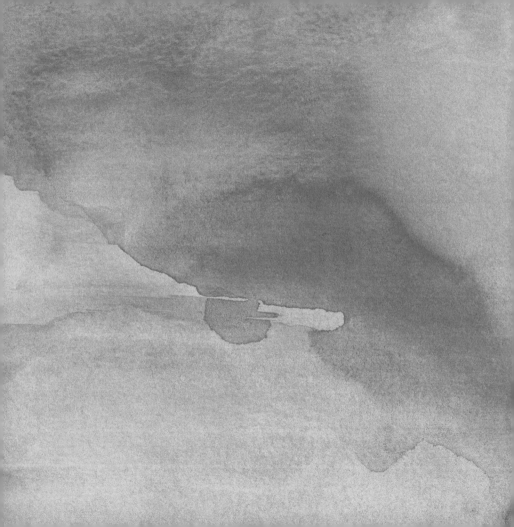

PHYSICAL TOUCH

1. SOAK UP THE SUN

Lie on a blanket on a sunny day together. Sit on a bench or on the balcony and enjoy the warmth of the sun.

2. SOFA SNUGGLES

Hold hands, cuddle, or make a physical connection while watching TV.

3. KISS OF LOVE

Kiss them, just because. Stop and enjoy the moment.

4. GIVE THEM "PHYSICAL TOUCH" GIFT CARDS

Give them the gift of touch, guilt free. It could be a massage or even a few appointments with a physical therapist if your loved one is bothered by bodily aches and pains.

5. MEANINGFUL COMFORT

Take time to give them extra affection when they're feeling sad or vulnerable. If they're upset, always offer your physical comfort.

6. WRAP YOUR LOVE AROUND THEM

Buy them a warm and cozy blanket that surrounds them with an embodiment of your love.

7. DRAW THEM CLOSE

Put your arm around them as you walk or stand together.

8. SCRATCH THEIR BACK

Experiment with what they like—get to know their preferences.

9. OPEN DOORS FOR THEM

Look after them while you're out.

10. WINGMAN

Be physically close when they're dealing with difficult people or in a tricky situation.

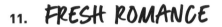

11. FRESH ROMANCE

Touch them the way you did when you were first dating. You'll feel like you're falling in love all over again!

12. BE THEIR SHELTER

Protect them from a cold wind. Offer them your coat or scarf on a chilly night.

13. RUN THEM A BATH

Light candles, put on music . . . create a place they can relax and unwind.

14. P.D.A.

Hold hands or put your arm around them while you're out—show them and others that they are your treasure.

15. STROKE THEIR HAIR

A gentle caress of their head, playing with the hair at the nape of their neck, or running your fingers through their hair and massaging their scalp—find out what touch they love most.

16. DANCE PARTNERS

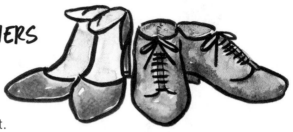

Take a dance class together. Find a YouTube teacher if time or money is tight.

17. STROKE THEIR NECK OR BACK

A tender touch that shows your love and affection.

18. MAKE TIME JUST TO CUDDLE

Give them a safe space to relax in your arms and show them your love without expecting anything more.

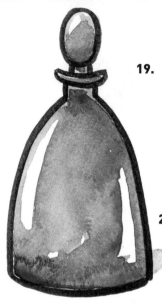

19. GIVE THEM A MASSAGE

Relieve their stiff muscles by rubbing their shoulders, back, neck, hands, or feet. Ask them what they like. Even five minutes can make a big difference to how they feel.

20. "TOUCHING" GIFTS

Buy them something tactile—a massage pillow, furry slippers, super-soft (or cotton-crisp, depending on their preference) bedsheets.

21. KISS THEM HELLO AND GOODBYE

Make coming and going a moment of tenderness and connection.

WORDS OF AFFIRMATION

	Date	*	Notes
1 2 3			
4 5 6			
7 8 9			
10 11 12			
13 14 15			
16 17 18			
19 20 21			

QUALITY TIME

	Date	*	Notes
1 2 3			
4 5 6			
7 8 9			
10 11 12			
13 14 15			
16 17 18			
19 20 21			

GIFTS

	Date	*	Notes
1 2 3			
4 5 6			
7 8 9			
10 11 12			
13 14 15			
16 17 18			
19 20 21			

ACTS OF SERVICE

	Date	*	Notes
1 2 3			
4 5 6			
7 8 9			
10 11 12			
13 14 15			
16 17 18			
19 20 21			

PHYSICAL TOUCH

	Date	*	Notes
1 2 3			
4 5 6			
7 8 9			
10 11 12			
13 14 15			
16 17 18			
19 20 21			

Find more (uncommon) ways
to connect with those you love.

Get ideas for fun, creative, and
spiritually engaging dates from
this unique resource.

978-0-8024-1174-7

Brings you fun, original
ideas for family time that
are affordable, manageable,
and enjoyable.

978-0-8024-1939-2

52 fun dates that help you
reinvigorate your relationship
and de-stress together.

978-0-8024-1938-5

Also available as eBooks